Between Gourmet Dinners and Ration Cards – Spotlight on the political economy of food security

2nd edition (AMAZON Kindle Publication Date: May 7, 2012), © 2012 by Glenn Brigaldino

The arguments in a nutshell

- The global food system is badly broken and is failing millions of people around the world. Food insecurity occurs not only in Africa and Asia, it also exists in the USA where food stamp usage is at an all-time high.

- Since the onset of the 2008 financial turmoil and the bail-out of the global speculators a flurry of international summits and conferences have seemingly catapulted food security to the top of aid donors' policy agendas. This has not prevented the 2011 food emergencies in the Horn of Africa, nor significantly reduced food insecurity in other parts of the world: globally about one billion people remain food insecure.

- Fundamental changes to the economics of how food is produced, consumed, distributed and shared are called for in order to anchor food security as a political priority at the global level. Food insecure people and their democratic movements and organizations need to be involved in planning and implementing food security policies and measures.

- Policy decisions made today, affect what kind of food security scenarios will prevail in the near future. In this sense, attaining food security emerges as a fundamentally political enterprise.

More than nuts and grains

For grocery shoppers around the world, filling up their carts or baskets with sufficient nutritious food is nowadays rarely an enjoyable experience. Selecting a variety of quality produce more often than not has been reduced to a tight financial balancing act. Whether filling up grocery bags in the neighborhood super market or bargaining with street vendors, consumers now walk away with either less groceries or these cost quite a lot more than just last year or the year before. Of course, food is rarely completely unavailable, even in the direst of human circumstances. Access and distribution mechanisms are always key factors when it comes to feeding people, whether through our air-conditioned multi-aisle super-markets or at roadside markets in an urban slum.

Crisis situations tend to emerge when the number of people able to fully meet their dietary needs steeply rises, not primarily because of logistical challenges to bring food to them but due to their prolonged inability to afford the food on the shelves or on the market tables. Free markets are inherently biased in favour of the better-off.

Ration card life

Years ago as a young field officer for the United Nations High Commissioner for Refugees (UNHCR), I was assigned to oversee care and maintenance operations in the refugee camps of northern Somalia. It was an eye-opening experience to say the least. At the time it was estimated that some 370 000 refugees lived in the regions' camps. The UN was responsible for protecting the refugees and for providing for their 'care and maintenance'. This included food and water, but also basic health care, shelter, education and various forms of simple social services. Official estimates suggested that there were some 840 000 refugees in all of Somalia. However it didn't take long to discover first-hand how inflated those numbers were. In spite of various attempts to physically count the refugee population, results were never made official. The simple reason being, that the Government at the time, the Siaad Barre dictatorship insisted in keeping the numbers confidential. Not only would the numbers have shown that at no time had there ever been more than perhaps 500 000 refugees in the country: questions would have arisen as to who was skimming off international assistance for some 340 000 phantom refugees.

The international community very well knew that the regime was funneling these resources to its own clan and supporters: it was the 'price to pay' in order to be allowed access to the actual refugees and most of all, for Somalia aligning itself with the "western camp' after a pro-soviet regime had toppled the archaic, feudal Ethiopian state ruled by emperor Haile Selassie. This had led to the USA losing its bases in Ethiopia and in order to maintain a 'regional counter balance' Somalia was swayed by political and economic promises to switch allegiances. So they did, and they threw the Russians out, who then crossed over to the now Eastern-block friendly Ethiopia while the Americans set up shop in Somalia. Neither the Russians nor the Americans helped in bringing food security to either of the countries, but they did dump large arsenals of weapons into the Horn of Africa.

In the case of Somalia, buying the Barre-regime's loyalty was also done through the humanitarian aid programs, notably by providing vast amounts of food aid from the US. Much more food was delivered than required for the number of genuine refugees, with the surplus going to the ruling clan and its supporters to be sold in local markets. This diversion of food aid took place at many levels. In the camps for example, camp commanders and their families, who were oftentimes formerly nomadic Somalis who had settled in the camps and were not refugees from Ethiopia, usually owned dozens, if not a few hundred refugee ration cards.

1

With the ration cards they were entitled to receive not only food, but also non-food items such as tents, utensils and tools. This skimming off of supplies which were intended for the actual refugees in need, in particular non-Somali, largely Christian Ethiopian refugees, meant that these people had to make do with reduced, below-survival rations. Control of the ration cards determined who had access to sufficient food. The actual amount of available food, while often fluctuating, was not the main factor in the allocation process.

Food shocks, laissez-faire

Still today and in countless other localities, the way food is controlled, distributed and allocated to food-insecure people is of greater relevance for feeding populations than is the actual process of growing and producing food.

Simply stated,

"In a world of plenty, a huge number go hungry. Hunger is more than just the result of food production and meeting demands. The causes of hunger are related to the causes of poverty. One of the major causes of hunger is poverty itself." (1)

The economic shock-turned-crisis of early 2008 disrupted the lives and livelihoods of millions of people all around the world and triggered an escalation of the structural, yet cyclical global food crisis. Soaring food prices and associated food riots in several developing countries attracted media attention and subsequently, food security was back on the agendas of politicians and self-proclaimed global leaders. It is not far-fetched to argue that the political uprisings across the Arab world are in part sparked by anger and desperation of millions of politically suppressed and economically marginalized people
living under food insecurity conditions or the threat thereof..

The tumultuous events in the Arab world might well be the land-based equivalent of the proverbial 'tip of the iceberg'. Already in 2008 the authors of an international report believed that

> "For the Least Developed Countries, … projections … show greatly increased vulnerability and uncertain food supplies during an era of high commodity prices and high price volatility." (2)

Round tables, distant plates

Since then there have been countless other reports, conferences, studies and food security initiatives. It is not easy to keep track of them or to make much practical sense of the sophisticated debates on causes of the food crisis. The technical and academic responses to contain and solve the crisis have so far been mostly inappropriate to reverse the crisis, not to speak of tackling the often political causes of entrenched, recurrent food insecurity.

Certainly, important insights and valuable advice have emerged from the intense discourse on food security or arguably, the absence thereof throughout our global commons. However by and large, policy responses have remained muffled in system-conformity, while the populations hardest hit by the food crisis, from Bangalore to Baltimore remain trapped in poverty and struggle to put food on the table for their families. Household strategies to cope with reduced access to food vary greatly and what works in an Indian village will not even be an option, say in a dilapidated urban area of Philadelphia. Undoubtedly, here as there those affected by food insecurity would welcome any form of high-level policy declarations that translated into concrete improvements of their daily lot.
Meanwhile, direct results are possible through local level responses to food insecurity conditions, for example urban agriculture has great potential, as has been demonstrated in Chicago, where a case study finds that

> "With access to land and water, the city's poor could cultivate their own vegetables to diversify their diets and achieve higher food security." (3)

In developing countries, significant and relatively quick inroads to reduced food insecurity can be made when smallholder and subsistence farmers are directly supported, for example through free agricultural inputs or cash and voucher programs.
The importance of support to these farmers is underscored by the fact that

> "three quarters of the poor people in developing countries live in rural areas and most of them reside on small farms....These small farmers include half the world's undernourished people." (4)

3

© 2008, Glenn Brigaldino

And while little if any food goes to waste among the hungry, measures aimed at food   producers can have rather immediate positive impacts on the amount of food that reaches markets. Recently the FAO reported that

> "The causes of food losses and waste in low-income countries are mainly connected to financial, managerial and technical limitations in harvesting techniques, storage and cooling facilities in difficult climatic conditions, infrastructure, packaging and marketing systems." (5)

Yet while short-term improvements are certainly feasible through a variety of technical fixes, serious challenges to the political factors underlying the "difficult conditions and systems" are called for and unquestionably, long overdue.

High-level action or actionism?

There is no denying that the countries dominating the global economy, and in particular those of the G8 have shown a remarkable burst of policy activity related to global food issues.

Some of the most prominent events with resulting policy declarations were:

- o **June 2008**: Global Food Summit in Rome; adopted declaration to increase assistance in particular for the least-developed countries and those that are most negatively affected by high food prices.
- o **July 2008**: €1 billion EU Food Facility announced
- o **Jan. 2009**: European Parliament issued a report calling for more European initiatives to ensure global food security.
- o **26-27 Jan. 2009**: UN "Food Security for All" meeting in Madrid
- o **4 March 2009**: Global food security conference in Prague.
- o **17-18 March 2009**: 2nd Forum for the Future of Agriculture: "The Global Financial and Economic Crisis: The challenge of financing food and environmental security"
- o **16-22 March 2009**: Fifth World Water Forum in Istanbul; featured sessions on 'Water and Food for ending Poverty and Hunger'
- o **12-13 Oct. 2009**: How to Feed the World in 2050: High-level expert forum in Rome.
- o **16-18 Nov. 2009**: World Summit on Food Security in Rome.
- o **28-31 March 2010**: Global Conference on Agricultural Research for Development, Montpellier.
- o **17 - 22 October 2011**, Committee on World Food Security (CFS) 37th Session, Rome.

However, as the Oakland Institute has noted,

"The plethora of international summits and declarations on the food price crisis between 2007 and 2009 may have prepared the ground for more effective food and agriculture policies in the future. However two years after the rise in food prices, it is hard to see much tangible result for the 1 billion hungry people." (6)

Undoubtedly, the amount of research and policy formulation that has resulted from these international efforts is impressive, both in terms of academic quality and positive political attention drawn to the often complex debates surrounding food security issues. Obviously coherence of strategies and coordination of initiatives and approaches remains an enormous organizational challenge.

In this regard, too much effort might turn out to be counter-productive as keeping track of which initiatives are being effectively implemented and dove-tail with other development polices can prove to be administratively cumbersome and politically confusing.

Although it is very helpful to depict international responses to global hunger in a single graphic (7), very few of the "hungry millions" will be less hungry as a consequence of policy declarations that do little to unsettle a global food and agricultural system that is wed to corporate interests and fossil fuels.

And it is more than doubtful if many of the policy- and declaration makers can systematically relate the numerous initiatives to one another: who can say whether the Evian declaration builds on the GPAFS process and reflects the Accra agenda while aiming to reach the MDG deadline with the support of the L'Aquila food security initiative? Maybe some experts can lay things out in plain language, just maybe.

World hunger and the international community's response

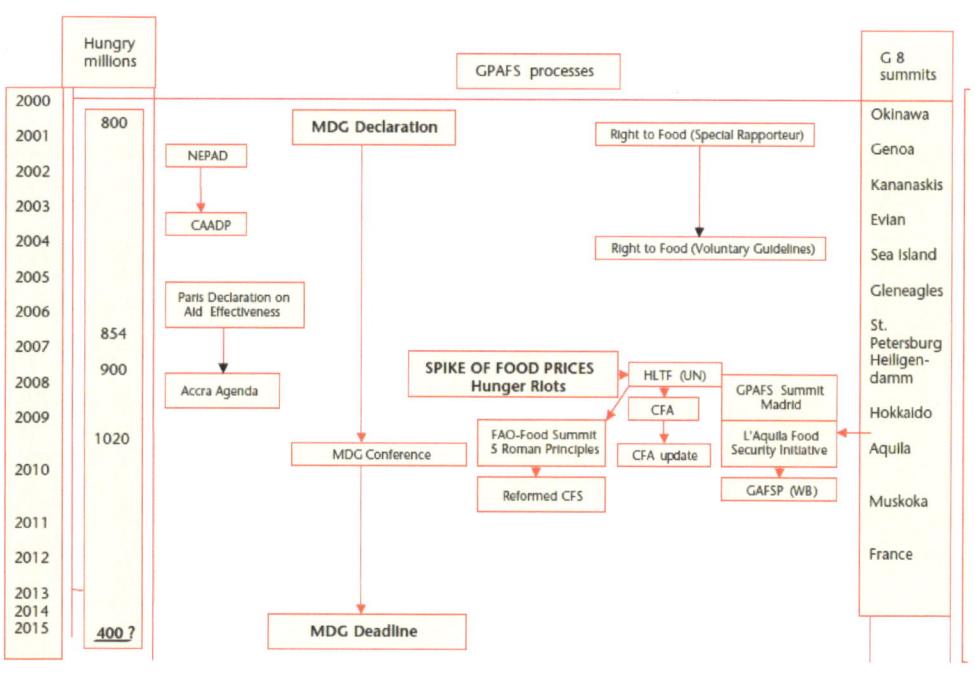

Source: **Dr Claus Auer,** *Rural 21 – 05/2010*

Debate, expert discussions and high-level deliberations continued at the meeting of the G20 agriculture ministers in Paris on 22-23 June 2011, "resulting", in a communiqué. (8)

6

Regrettably this event too can be seen as a missed opportunity.

The "watered down communiqué" has been described as making only largely technical efforts,

"… contain(ing) only vague references to some of the most difficult issues facing agricultural producers in developing countries. While the G20 nations largely agree on the need to improve agricultural productivity and enhance transparency, they disagree on biofuels, export controls and on the regulation of commodities and financial markets. ….. It would appear that we will have to face another food price crisis before the world's most influential nations get serious about tackling the really tough issues."

In light of the ongoing severe food crisis in the Horn of Africa, much more than a price crisis is upon us, as a return to the devastating peak in famine conditions of 2011 cannot be ruled out by those issuing food policy communiqués. (9)

It appears that business as usual is the name of the game for the world's rich and their political friends in high places. Many of them met at the 2012 regional World Economic Forum (WEF) on Africa, held in Addis Ababa, Ethiopia in May 2012. In a WEF commissioned paper on agriculture, there is no mention of how the prevailing global food system is at the heart of food insecurity across the globe.

Instead, a 'new vision to deliver economic growth and opportunity' is called for, the usual lip-service to 'partnership' and inclusion of stakeholders is paid, while a firm, deeply ideological, 'free market' belief in the commitment of 'government leaders' to implement policies in support of food security persists. (10)

Such a belief in existing leaders might not always be misplaced, but it ignores the ample evidence, notably in Ethiopia, that the very leaders called upon to enact pro-poor development, are often the same, democratically unaccountable despots who use food as a weapon in support of their personal, and politically narrow agendas. (11) Sadly, or rather to the shame of the leaders of the G8 'free world' (and insulting to anyone seriously concerned about the pain suffered by food insecure people), the Ethiopian ruler Meles Zenawi was again invited to attend a G8 summit, this time in Camp David 2012.

The Human Rights Watch on 'Forced Displacement and 'Villagization' in Ethiopia'
will most certainly not be slipped into the conference reader the forum participants will be flipping through in their 329 sq. ft / 30m² club rooms with butler service for $279 a night at the Addis Ababa Sheraton Hotel. Conveniently for them, the chances are slim that they will encounter any impoverished, under-nourished food-insecure locals in the hotel lobby or at the event: the 5000 Swiss francs event registration fee works an effective deterrent.

-

No-food nations

A radical departure from the system-conformity of nation-state decision-makers, is not unthinkable. In fact it is being practiced everyday by millions of food insecure people around the world. Populations living under authoritarian rule or within fragile state structures often depend on uncertain international relief responses to meet their food needs. Important as they are, such short-term food aid relief efforts are generally a symptom of a failed nation-state, one unable or unwilling to protect the livelihoods of its own people(s). Indeed, in such cases the nation-state is part of the problem and not a genuine stakeholder in solving the food security problems of its citizens.

It is well-worth reflecting on Raj Patel's statement that "The opposite of greed isn't thrift it's generosity" (see video clip at http://rajpatel.org/2010/07/28/the-value-of-nothing-2).

In his book 'Stuffed and Starved', Patal asserts that there is a simultaneous existence of nearly 1 billion people who are malnourished and nearly 1 billion who are overweight: a fact that is an inevitable corollary of a global economic system where a handful of corporations have been allowed to capture the value of the food chain. (12)

In parallel to this trend towards corporate penetration of the global food supply, a 'new wave of accumulation by dispossession in Africa' has occurred, with still unknown longer-term consequences to food security on the continent. More and more land deals are being struck in Africa with firms from around the world, notably from China and India. The role of the African state in the process is pivotal, as the terms of the deals struck often appear more favorable to the ruling, undemocratic elites, including donor darlings such as Ethiopia, than to the millions of food insecure who experience reduced access to or even dispossession from quality land. (13)

Participatory approaches towards improving food security in many developing countries are gaining some ground and are discussed under the food sovereignty paradigm. This affirms

"the fundamental right of peoples to define their food and agricultural policies (and) implies that food providers and consumers are *directly* involved in framing policies for food, agriculture, livelihoods and the environment. (It argues) that existing decision-making and policy processes that are based on models of representative democracy are **inadequate** for transformation towards food sovereignty. (14)

Meanwhile, the main international donor countries do not appear to be making any significant adjustments to their aid and relief policies. In fact it is easy to argue that the very policies and remedies they propose to countries facing massive food and environmental turmoil, have proven to be flawed and failing in the donor countries themselves. With unemployment at stubbornly high levels, poverty rates worrisome and financial systems under tremendous pressure, it should come as no surprise that food insecurity is also widespread in many donor countries.

In the USA,

"…there are now almost 46 million people ….on food stamps, roughly 15 percent of the population. That's an increase of 74 percent since 2007, just before the financial crisis and a deep recession led to mass job losses." (15)

At home as abroad, food aid donors such as the USA and the EU countries remain silent
with regard to

"…the causes of the food crisis, and the increasingly hard-to-ignore critiques and consequences of a deeply undemocratic and crisis-prone process of food system globalization". (16)

Indeed the pattern of aid to developing countries since the late 1980s has been reflective of the rise of globalization as the organizing principle for capitalist production, also in the agricultural sector and the fossil fuel dependent global food system.

It is a well-known fact that 'fossil fuels are essential for modern, mechanized agricultural production systems and that food production is energy intensive'. Looking ahead to fossil fuel resources decreasing and to an 'end to cheap oil' food security faces new risks in the absence of significant incentive to reduce fossil fuels in agriculture and to introduce sustainable alternative production and distribution systems (alongside changes in consumption patterns). (17)

Aid to agriculture in sub-Saharan Africa has been falling dramatically as a proportion of all aid, now hovering around 3 to 4% compared to over 16% in 1980. In parallel, aid to agriculture "has been used to dismantle state interventions in agriculture, including states' ability to regulate markets effectively." (18)

While at the bilateral level there appears to be little movement to abandon pro-elite and anti-poor free-market ideology, within the UN system some frank critique has been expressed. UNCTAD has stated that "Market fundamentalist laissez-fair of the last 20 years has dramatically failed the test", going on to conclude with regard to the excesses of global financial speculation that have shaken the world economy and resulted in bail-outs financed by the average working class citizens, that

"Nothing short of closing the big casino will provide a lasting solution". (19)

So while the state of "Food Security in the World" remains dismal, notably in protracted crisis situations as in the Horn of Africa and the number of under-nourished people hovers around or above one billion, different scenarios and their implications of food security and sustainable human development need to be contemplated. (20)

Indeed global food security must be seen as a core element of an overall global social crises resulting from a continued laissez faire approach to socio-economic development, alongside eroded democratic institutions and representation mechanisms, notably in the core capitalist countries. Yet while "Fundamental problems in the global food production and trading system must be addressed to ensure sustained food security" the attention paid by political leaders to "the fragile and unsustainable global food security" situations in most major industrialized countries has increasingly been replaced by budget cuts and fiscal austerity responses to the protracted, financial and economic crises. In the meantime the need shift in developing countries "from predominantly export-oriented agricultural policies .... to strengthen(ed) domestic food production to better meet local needs for affordable food and to cushion the impact of international price shocks remains on hold". (21)

Crises today, climate insecurity tomorrow

As I have argued elsewhere, fundamentally re-imagining the global food economy is the basis for lasting improvements in global food security. The political responses to the recurring failures of the global food system, even commendable relief and project-level responses to the immediate hardships faced by food-insecure populations, perhaps allow for some temporary reprieve from an ongoing, livelihoods debilitating crisis. Yet root causes of the crisis are hardly touched in the process. (22)

Given that food emergences are largely responded to with massive, although rarely sufficiently large relief efforts, early warning efforts have frequently been frustrated by lackluster political commitment to provide assistance before the onset of a full-scale food crisis. Clearly there is no shortage of research and timely analysis and early warning data: even satellite-based imagery is only a mouse-click away. (23)

It seems as if for too many citizens in the richer, more affluent countries (where obesity concerns are a worrying dimension of homegrown nutritional problems) food emergencies and hunger events around the world are seen as natural events, reoccurring in poor countries in regular intervals. Long-term prevention seems next to impossible where such a mindset becomes entrenched and consequently, responses leading to genuine solutions tend to be neglected by aid donors and governments in food insecure countries alike.

Changes in climate patterns and possible consequences for future food security conditions are a case in point. Very few people spend any time imagining how climate change by 2050 will be altering growing patterns and crop yields in today's' already food insecure countries. Growing seasons are expected to shift, the types of crops that can grow effectively in a region are likely to change and existing agriculture practices, both cultural and economic ones are bound to be upset. Ingenuity and creative long-term planning is called for to foster sustainable forms of agriculture, as well as to enable sustainable rural and urban livelihoods that can guarantee stable food security conditions. (24)

Considerable uncertainties persist in the agricultural sector and at national, regional and global levels the agricultural sector is marred by distortive price support and subsidy schemes, as well as corporation-friendly trade policies.

Meanwhile evidence mounts that changing climate patterns in one part of the world impact rainfall levels in food insecure regions elsewhere, in particular where agriculture is predominantly rain-fed as in the Horn of Africa. Using observations and climate model simulations, climate scientists have been able to link the decreased East African rainfall to abrupt changes in sea-surface temperatures in the tropical Pacific Ocean. (25)

It is as of yet unclear if sea-surface temperature changes are in any way related to the problem of accumulation of plastic waste floating in the Pacific Ocean, infamously referred to as the 'Great Pacific Garbage Patch'. (26) On the other hand, there is little doubt among oceanographers, that the observed melting of the Greenland ice sheet raises the risk of increased fresh water release into the Atlantic. Not only could this result in rising sea levels, it could disruptively impact upon the global ocean circulation system and eventually disrupt the relatively mild climate in Europe, with consequences for high-productivity agricultural production there. (27)

The linkages between food security, food production systems and natural resources and climate change are complex and not necessarily obvious. It is important to point out that

"Short-term plans to address food insecurity, provide access to water resources, or encourage economic growth must be placed in the context of future climate change, to ensure that short-term activities in a particular area do not increase vulnerability to climate change in the long term." (28)

Political climate, food security horizons

Much more fundamental review and debate, reaching far beyond technical fixes and uncritical, market-based production and distribution policies and mechanisms are direly needed. Nothing short of a full rethinking of "the future of food" is called for. Chatham House, a leading UK-based think tank, has spelled out an outstanding example of what such a rethink encompasses. Four scenarios are presented which

"...illustrate a range of circumstances that food supply actors in both developed and developing countries must expect to face in the years to come. These are not predictions of the future. But they are reasoned depictions that are being used to provoke thinking and engage stakeholders in debate.... Across the world the responses to change will be conditioned by uncertainties surrounding the availability of sufficient energy, water, land and skills".

In brief, the four global food supply scenarios are:

- 'Just a Blip': *the.... high price of food proves to be a brief spike with a return*
  to cheap food at some point soon
- 'Food Inflation': *food prices remain high for a decade or more*
- 'Into a New Era': *today's food system has reached its limits and must change*
- 'Food in Crisis': *a major world food crisis develops.* (29)

It is probably safe to assume that the first scenario, is no longer realistic and in my own opinion, with the escalation of the food crisis in the Horn of Africa, alongside globally increasing food prices, we are currently oscillating in as yet undefined territory, somewhere in between the other three scenarios.

It does not seem as a feasible option, or ethically justifiable that the foundations of today's food system structure remain unchanged.

While there are countless local, regional and household-level efforts directed at changing a globalization-driven economic system that continuously fails to ensure food security for everyone, these efforts have yet to establish a durable, parallel mode of economic interaction at the national level and beyond.

Non-conformist efforts are not immune from the recurring economic shocks, crises and disasters triggered and perpetuated by the dominating system of unaccountable, market driven mechanisms which largely determine global food production, distribution and consumption patterns, frequently irrespective of human basic needs and environmental impacts.

However they can serve as important steps alongside

" Wider structural changes...needed to ensure the global food system can meet the needs of a growing population and the needs of those who produce the world's food. A food system that is not shaped by unjust trade rules and a handful of powerful corporations, but instead supports ecologically sustainable small-scale food producers...
Regulating agricultural commodity markets alone will not tackle the many challenges of global food production. But in the wake of the financial crisis, there is a unique opportunity to introduce financial market regulation, taking the first steps to improving the global food system for the benefit of food producers and consumers." (30)

Democratic political struggles alongside societal preparedness to abandon consumerist lifestyles could be a powerful force of change. The protests in 2011 under the Occupy banner and 'We are the 99%' sent shockwaves through the complacent mainstream defenders and the elites of pro-market laissez-faire capitalism and its business-as-usual crisis management approaches.

At least for 2012, the business-as-usual gathering of the G8 was obliged to re-locate. Plans to hold the G-8 economic summit in Chicago were ditched on short notice as the US instead chose to host 'world leaders' at the presidential retreat at Camp David in Maryland. The Chicago host committee had estimated it could have cost $40 million to $65 million to stage the event, including the costs for security. So far there has been no word whether or not the money saved, will go to any Chicago food banks or anti-poverty groups.

The Occupy protests to date mark a crucial step forward in linking disparate and often only loosely associated democratic political multitudes. Commonalities among them exist in their genuine opposition to the entrenched economic system: a system that is synonymous with the political failure to ensure food security and which is responsible for constantly deepening inequalities around the world.

As the system continues to fail and crumble, today's policy-makers, those who perpetuate the endurance of an economic system incapable of granting food security for all, could then find themselves gathered around an empty table when they convene for one of their next choreographed summits.

Glenn Brigaldino is an independent political analyst.
He is based in Ottawa, Canada.

References:

(1) Anup Shah, 2010: Causes of Hunger are related to Poverty at:
http://www.globalissues.org/article/7/causes-of-hunger-are-related-to-poverty#globalissues-org

(2)   OECD-FAO, Agricultural Outlook 2008-2017
http://www.oecd.org/dataoecd/54/15/40715381.pdf

also see:
OECD-FAO AGRICULTURAL OUTLOOK, 2011-2020, Part I, report flyer at
http://www.fao.org/fileadmin/user_upload/newsroom/docs/Outlookflyer.pdf
full report at
http://www.agri-outlook.org/pages/0,2987,en_36774715_36775671_1_1_1_1_1,00.html

(3) Corinne Kisner, December 2008: Green Roofs for Urban Food Security and
Environmental Sustainability - URBAN AGRICULTURE CASE STUDY: CHICAGO,
ILLINOIS,
http://www.climate.org/topics/international-action/urban-agriculture/chicago.htm
also see: Growing Power's Chicago Projects,
http://www.growingpower.org/chicago_projects.htm

(4) Action Aid, 2008: Failing the rural poor
http://www.actionaid.gr/files/File/Downloads/failing_the_rural_poor_actionaid_report.pdf

(5) FAO, 2011: Global food losses and food waste – Extent, Causes and Prevention, Robert
van Otterdijk and Alexandre Meybeck; the authors note that in industrialized countries,
"Consumer households need to be informed and change the behavior which causes the
current high levels of food waste."
http://www.fao.org/fileadmin/user_upload/ags/publications/GFL_web.pdf

(6) Mousseau, F., 2010: The High Food Price Challenge: A Review of Responses to
Combat Hunger; The Oakland Institute
http://www.oaklandinstitute.org/pdfs/high_food_prices_web_final.pdf

The Report of the Foresight Global Food and Farming Futures Project makes a strong case
for governments, the private sector and civil society to continue to prioritize global food
security, sustainable agricultural production and fisheries, reform of trade and subsidy,
waste reduction and sustainable consumption. It "explore the pressures on the global food
system between now and 2050 and identify the decisions that policy makers need to take
today".

http://webarchive.nationalarchives.gov.uk/+/http://www.bis.gov.uk/foresight/our-work/projects/current-projects/global-food-and-farming-futures/reports-and-publications

(7) Claus Auer, 2010: Global Partnership for Agriculture and Food Security:
Actors, missions and achievements, in: Rural 21 – 05/2010
http://www.rural21.com/1322.html

(8) The communiqué "ACTION PLAN ON FOOD PRICE VOLATILITY AND AGRICULTURE" can be found at
http://www.g20.utoronto.ca/2011/2011-agriculture-plan-en.pdf

John Thompson's critique of the 28 June 2011 meeting "A missed opportunity…" is posted at http://www.future-agricultures.org/index.php?option=com_easyblog&view=entry&id=50&Itemid=473

Note from his critique: The Group of Twenty (G20), comprised of the world's 19 largest economies, plus the European Union, was created as a response both to the financial crises of the late 1990s and to a growing recognition that key emerging-market countries were not adequately included in the core of global economic discussion and governance. Collectively, the G20 countries account for 85% of global gross national product, 80% of world trade and 66% of the world population.

Elsewhere, it has been said that expecting 'summeteers' and their pro-globalization institutions like the World Bank and the IMF to solve the problems underlying food insecurity is like "asking an arsonist to put out a forest fire".

Sam Urquhart, Making a Profit Out of the Food Crisis, in Toward Freedom, 16 July 2008
http://www.towardfreedom.com/globalism/1356-making-a-profit-out-of-the-food-crisis-from-a-brave-new-world-bank-to-monsanto

(9) The USAID-funded Famine Early Warning Systems Network (FEWS NET) monitors and analyzes food security and produces monthly food security reports. In its August 2011 update it reports that in Ethiopia alone about 4.8 million people (including an estimated 250,000 refugees from Somalia, South Sudan and Eritrea) continue to require assistance.
http://www.fews.net/pages/country.aspx?gb=et

(10) World Economic Forum 2011, Putting the New Vision for Agriculture into Action: A transformation is happening,
http://www.weforum.org/reports/putting-new-vision-agriculture-action-transformation-happening

(11) "'Waiting Here for Death': Forced Displacement and 'Villagization' in Ethiopia's Gambella Region," examines the first year of Gambella's villagization program. It details the involuntary nature of the transfers, the loss of livelihoods, the deteriorating food situation, and ongoing abuses by the armed forces against the affected people. Many of the areas from which people are being moved are slated for leasing by the government for commercial agricultural development.

Human Rights Watch, 2012
http://www.hrw.org/reports/2012/01/16/waiting-here-death

(12) Raj Patel Stuffed and Starved: Markets, Power and the Hidden Battle for the World's Food System, Portobello, 2008, http://rajpatel.org/2009/10/27/stuffed-and-starved
Reviewed by Felicity Lawrence at:
http://www.guardian.co.uk/books/2007/sep/15/healthmindandbody.health

(13) See thematic issue of Review of African Political Economy (ROAPE), Land: a new wave of accumulation by dispossession in Africa, no. 128, 2011; in the same issue, see Toward Freedom contributor Glenn Brigaldino's briefing "Elections in the imperial periphery: Ethiopia hijacked" which also touches upon land deals there.
http://www.tandfonline.com/doi/abs/10.1080/03056244.2011.582768

For further news reports about the global rush to buy up or lease farmlands abroad as a strategy to secure basic food supplies or simply for profit, see: http://farmlandgrab.org

(14) International Institute for Environment and Development, 2010, Chapter 5 Reclaiming citizenship - empowering civil society in policy-making by Michel Pimbert in Towards Food Sovereignty http://pubs.iied.org/G02612.html?c=agric/food

The FAO facilitated Global Forum on Food Security and Nutrition (FSN Forum) seeks to include outside views and voices in discussing the global food system and policies. It currently consists of more than 3200 members from across the world's five continents.
http://km.fao.org/fsn

(15) See: USA becomes Food Stamp Nation but is it sustainable?, by Kristina Cooke, Reuters – Mon, Aug 22, 2011
http://news.yahoo.com/usa-becomes-food-stamp-nation-sustainable-160645036.html

The charity 'Feeding America' produces the 'Map the Meal Gap' interactive map which presents a state by state overview of where US residents are struggling with hunger. In many places, close to 20% of the population are affected.
http://feedingamerica.org/~/link.aspx?_id=12F7FAA41CEE49A49001479D15BEB032&_z=z

(16) From an aid sustainability perspective, Jamey Essex calls for "closer attention to and integration of critiques…as articulated not only by aid experts and practitioners, but by social movement groups representing…peasants and small farmers."

Jamey Essex, Sustainability, Food Security, and Development Aid after the Food Crisis: Asssessing Aid Strategies across Donor Contexts, in: *Sustainability* 2010, *2*(11), 3354-3382, full text at: http://www.mdpi.com/2071-1050/2/11/3354

(17) UNEP Global Environmental Alert Service (GEAS), April 2012, The end to cheap oil: a threat to food security and an incentive to reduce fossil fuels in agriculture
http://na.unep.net/geas/getUNEPPageWithArticleIDScript.php?article_id=81

(18) ActionAid International, 2008: Failing the rural poor - Aid, Agriculture and the Millennium Development Goals
http://www.actionaid.org.uk/doc_lib/failing_the_rural_poor_actionaid_report.pdf

(19) United Nations Conference on Trade and development (UNCTAD), 2009, The Global Economic Crisis: Systemic failures and multilateral remedies
http://www.unctad.org/en/docs/gds20091_en.pdf

(20) In 2010 the UN's food organizations FAO and WFP published their "Food Security in the World" report http://www.un-ngls.org/spip.php?article3063

and the World Watch Institute has presented its 2011 "State of the World – Innovations that nourish the planet" report. It identifies three challenges that are central to the global conversation on hunger reduction and that need to be addressed:

- Unify the food security, climate change, and ecosystem protection agendas
- Rise above conflicting perspectives on the causes and solutions to hunger
- Empower farmers and communities to feed themselves.

http://www.worldwatch.org/sow11

(21) United Nations, Department of Economic and Social Affairs, 2011, The Global Social Crisis - Report on the World Social Situation 2011
http://social.un.org/index/ReportontheWorldSocialSituation/2011.aspx

(22) Brigaldino, Glenn, Book Review of 'The Global Food Economy - The battle for the future of farming", by Tony Weis (London & New York: Zed Books 2007) in: Review of African Political Economy, 2008 no. 118: 689-690
http://www.tandfonline.com/doi/abs/10.1080/03056240802574318

Tony Weis' excellent and very readable book is available at
http://www.amazon.com/Global-Food-Economy-Battle-Farming/dp/1842777955

(23) Through its Global Information and Early Warning System (GIEWS), the UN provides excellent early warnings of impending food crises in individual countries. The FAO/GIEWS and the World Food Programme also carry out joint Crop and Food Security Assessment Missions (CFSAMs). Their purpose is to provide timely and reliable information so that appropriate actions can be taken by the governments, the international community, and other parties. http://www.fao.org/giews

(24) M.Burke, D. Lobell and L. Guarino in: Global Environmental Change, 19 (2009) 317-325, Shifts in African crop climates by 2050 and the implications for crop improvement and genetic resources conservation
(25) B. Lyon and D. DeWitt, A recent and abrupt decline in the East African long rains, in: GEOPHYSICAL RESEARCH LETTERS, VOL. 39, 2012
 http://www.agu.org/pubs/crossref/2012/2011GL050337.shtml

(26) Glenn Brigaldino, Garbage Imports, Global Plastic, Yahoo! Contributor Network, 2009; http://voices.yahoo.com/garbage-imports-global-plastic-4086497.html?cat=7

(27) Christian Rodehacke and his fellow scientists at the Max Planck Institute for Meteorology explore numerous aspects of the ocean's role in climate dynamics, including the interactions between ice sheets and the climate system.

http://www.mpimet.mpg.de/en/science/the-ocean-in-the-earth-system/ocean-physics/interaction-between-ice-sheets-and-climate-system.html

For a general yet solid explanation of large-scale ocean circulation, see: Wikipedia thermohaline circulation, http://en.wikipedia.org/wiki/Thermohaline_circulation

(28) Eva Ludi, ODI Background Note March 2009, Climate change, water and food security
http://www.odi.org.uk/resources/details.asp?id=3148&title=climate-change-water-food-security

(29) Chatham House Food Supply Project, May 2008, Thinking About the Future of Food: The Chatham House Food Supply Scenarios
http://www.chathamhouse.org/publications/papers/view/108816

Also explore "FoodWeb 2020" and its report '*Forces Shaping the Future of Food*, which contains forecasts about directions of change and examples of disruptions in the food system as well as innovative responses to them.

http://www.iftf.org/FoodWeb2020Forces

(30) Murray Worthy, 2011: Broken markets: How financial market regulation can help prevent another global food, for World Development Movement
http://www.wdm.org.uk/stop-bankers-betting-food/broken-markets-how-financial-regulation-can-prevent-food-crisis

© 2012 by Glenn Brigaldino

Crumbs of capitalism for you and me

An original contribution to
Newtopiamagazine (January 2013)

"…a collective of artists and writers who will develop independent autonomous work in collaboration with other members, and gather related content from around the web."

http://newtopiamagazine.wordpress.com

Photo: © G.Brigaldino, 2012

Crumbs of capitalism for you and me
Glenn Brigaldino
© 2013

Our ruling class steers us into disaster after disaster, cheering for ruinous wars... But accountability, it seems, is something that applies only to people at the bottom....

Thomas Frank, Easy Chair, in:
Harper's, August 2012

The platitudes are not new. Only nowadays, they ring hollower than ever before: 'We are living above our means', 'When times are hard we all have to make sacrifices' or 'First things will get worse before they can get any better'. What was initially described as the financial crisis of 2008/09 is now described on Wikipedia as the '2007–2012 global financial crisis' (1) And what a crisis it is turning out to be, already half a decade long and with no end in sight. The Governments in rich and poor countries alike have struggled to contain the crisis but their policy fixes have done little to tackle the causes which are largely rooted in an intensified economic globalization that increasingly eludes attempts at political regulation or democratic accountability.

In 2010 protestors around the world joined 'Occupy Now!' campaigns, to voice their discontent and take political action to oppose the injustices and inequalities of the globalised capitalist system. In the USA it is election year and 'the economy' will be the 'front & centre' topic debated in the popular media. What the Occupy movement has highlighted, that rather than smart-talk and pseudo science about which economic models and strategies can 'turn things around' the real question to ask is 'who's' economy are we talking about?

This is essentially what is meant by 'political economy': what is an economic system based upon, how is it organized, who are the people controlling the economic system and what social forces exist or can be politically mobilized to ensure economic decisions benefit all of society and mot disproportionally a few of its privileged members.

Truly a taller order to discuss than the polished and intellectually limited debates that usually find their way into the broadcast superficial debates and the pretty charts that pass as analysis that are produced by the opinion pollsters.

Many of our mainstreamed TV commentators were quick to voice outcries of injustice when the French national assembly voted to tax the highest earners in the country at a rate of 75 per cent, following on a campaign promise made by recently elected President Francois Hollande.

The measure would affect earnings of more than €1 million ($1.27 million) per year but only for the next two years. It would be paid by an estimated 1500 people and provide the government with an extra €210 million ($267 million) in revenue per year.[i] If such an amount were made available in the US, it would be sufficient, assuming a lower-end average estimate of $750 a month, to cover daycare for over 350 000 children. That this any kids and many more do not have the chance to go to day care does not stir up any outcry from the aforementioned commentators.[ii]

The financial crisis cannot be meaningfully discussed or properly understood without situating the finance dimension of the economy into the much broader, systemic crisis of the global development model we have come to view as 'globalization'. A positive side-effect of the increased attention to the turmoil in global markets is the heightened awareness of economic in equalities and injustices throughout the world.

In the homeland of un-controlled capitalism, the numbers have been lop-sided for decades. In short:

"In the United States, wealth is highly concentrated in a relatively few hands. As of 2007, the top 1% of households (the upper class) owned 34.6% of all privately held wealth, and the next 19% (the managerial, professional, and small business stratum) had 50.5%, which means that just 20% of the people owned a remarkable 85%, leaving only 15% of the wealth for the bottom 80% (wage and salary workers)." (2)

As the crisis persists, governments become deeply dependent on the very financial institutions which have fed the global debt crisis with their insatiable hunger for ever-rising profits. Around the world we seem to be witnessing " ...the drama of democratic states being turned into debt-collecting agencies on behalf of a global oligarchy of investors", as

".. the markets' have begun to dictate in unprecedented ways what presumably sovereign and democratic states may still do for their citizens and what they must refuse them. The same Manhattan-based ratings agencies that were instrumental in bringing about the disaster of the global money industry are now threatening to downgrade the bonds of states that accepted a previously unimaginable level of new debt to rescue that industry and the capitalist economy as a whole." (3)

There are solid arguments is support of reversing of wealth accumulation amongst the numerical minuscule but politically nearly untouchable ultra-rich in North America. Indeed, the arguments for radical reversal of income inequality must be made at a global scale. But while the state once also played a buffering role through redistributive and welfare programs and acknowledgement of labour rights and demands, the state today is far less of an ally of the disadvantaged than it has been in decades.

While financial bailouts are created for those who regularly push the capitalist market to near-collapse, the low-waged, seniors and unemployed are those who are expected to jump off so-called fiscal cliffs.

This pattern of state retreat from the public and civil spheres of society in favor of the corporate and privileged spheres has become a globalised, thus deepening an already significant legitimacy deficit amongst the still formally democratic but increasingly semi-representative political systems especially in the richer countries of the North.

"... (W)ith the penetration of the market has come not a retreat of the State, but rather a shift in the State's priorities. States no longer prioritize being responsive and accountable to their populations, but rather increasingly look to protect and advance the interests of corporations and economies at the expense of society.

Neoliberal globalization has, moreover, not only intensified exploitation at the workplace and extended exploitation to the sphere of social reproduction, in such matters as health care and education; it has extended its own reach to the furthest corners of the global South."[iii]

However those with power and in control of society's political and economic institutions tend to be among the wealthy themselves and obviously have no interest in dismantling the towering podium they and their rich friends are comfortably sitting upon. Even as the global crisis deepens and spreads, the

"... trend in the U.S. and Canada to rising income inequality thus leads to periodic financial crises, greater volatility of aggregate income and, as governments respond to mass unemployment with counter-cyclical fiscal policies, a compounding instability of public finances. ..... The conundrum in all this inequality-induced macro-economic instability is that it clearly can be avoided. A steeply progressive income tax system can reduce the instability implications of increasing inequality .... Yet, in both the U.S. and Canada, the progressivity of the income tax system has been substantially eroded, over the same period in which the pre-tax incomes of the top 1% have grown most strongly. (4)

Even officially, the poverty rate for the U.S. stands at 15 percent for 2011. Poverty is greatest among children (21.9 percent), compared with seniors (8.7 percent) and working-age adults (13.7 percent)..... the median annual household income declined for the second year in a row, to $50,054 and thus, lower than it has been since 1996. [iv]

Indeed, as Sam Pizzigati has said, 'most Americans have essentially spent the last 20 years on a go-nowhere treadmill. They're working longer and harder and have zero new wealth to show for their labor.' (5)

To elaborate a bit on the case of Canada, the arguments in favor of a more equal society were largely acted upon in the past, when universal healthcare was introduced nationally and wage earners saw wage increases above annual inflation rates.

Those days are long gone and although many Canadians still believe that 'things are better here', there are few meaningful statistics to back- up such a feel-good psyche. For years, productivity and innovation rates in Canada have been falling as wage incomes remain below those in US.

Among peers, Canada is being noticed, for all the wrong reasons:

"Income inequality among working-age persons has been rising in Canada, particularly since the mid-1990s . .... and is above the OECD average. ... Moreover, that of the richest 0.1% more than doubled, from 2% to 5.3%. At the same time, the top federal marginal income tax rates saw a marked decline: dropping from 43% in 1981 to 29% in 2010. ... Taxes and benefits reduce inequality less in Canada than in most OECD countries. (6)

The numbers are there for anyone to read:

> "In OECD countries today, the average income of the richest 10% of the population is about nine times that of the poorest 10% – a ratio of 9 to 1. However, the ratio varies widely from one country to another. It is much lower than the OECD average in the Nordic and many continental European countries, but reaches 10 to 1 in Italy, Japan, Korea, and the United Kingdom; around 14 to 1 in Israel, Turkey, and the United States; and 27 to 1 in Mexico and Chile."

Recent OECD reports show that there is nothing inevitable about such unsettling, growing inequalities. However, being essentially a 'rich man's club' amongst the world's nations, the OECD is unable to prescribe any policies or even political strategies that could call for abandoning the free-market capitalist growth model the global rich thrive upon. Capsizing their own ship is not an option the 1% will ever contemplate.

The language of 'change' thus remains nebulous and mostly general in nature: "Globalisation and technological changes offer opportunities but also raise challenges that can be tackled with effective and well-targeted policies". As the global working classes continues to impoverish they are encourages to stay the course of free markets continuous economic shocks and downturns as somehow, the very system that unleashes these crisis, will miraculously self-correct itself.

One serious consequence of prolonged inequality that results from 'the war on salaries' is the erosion of health and life expectancy among the poorer segments of society. Simply speaking, the poor live less healthy and shorter lives than the rich.

(c) 2012, G.Brigaldino

Research published in the online journal 'Population Health Metrics' demonstrates that "during the period 2000 to 2007, life expectancy in the US and most of its counties fell behind the progress seen in other nations."

The authors go on to note that the

> "US has extremely large geographic and racial
> disparities, with some communities having life
> expectancies already well behind those of the best-
> performing nations. In 2007, life expectancy at birth for
> American men and women was 75.6 and 80.8 years,
> ranking 37th and 37th, respectively, in the world. Across
> US counties, life expectancy at birth ranged from 65.9 to
> 81.1 years for men and 73.5 to 86.0 years for women. ...
> The extent of geographic inequality is substantially larger
> in the US than in the UK, Canada, or Japan.

> In spite of the US maintaining ' its position as the country
> that spent the most per capita on health care throughout
> this period (2000-2007)." (7)

One would expect that very few of the <1% reside in a country
with a life expectancy of only 65.9 years.

From a public health perspective, it is no new phenomena that
those who are poor experience dismal health outcomes. The
trend is common in the world's poorest countries and regions.
There, as in the homeland of inequality-breeding capitalism, the
2008 global economic crisis has had a disturbing and sad effect
upon women and children.

Researchers at the Asian Development Bank have reported that

> "economic downturns tend to have stronger effects,
> especially for girls, than economic booms: life expectancy
> of girls and boys increases by an estimated 2 years during
> good economic periods but decreases by 7 years for girls,
> and 6 years for boys, during adverse economic times.

> There is "an average increase in infant mortality of 7.4
> deaths per 1000 births for girls compared with 1.5 deaths
> per 1000 births for boys for every one or more unit fall in
> Gross Domestic Product (GDP)." (8)

That inequality has no upsides for the poor goes without saying, and those within a society who tend to benefit when inequality levels are high and entrenched, cannot deny that

> "Inequality has the greatest impact on the poor and those living in the most deprived areas of society. Children do particularly badly in unequal societies – from worse infant mortality rates, through to lower levels of participation in further education. In more unequal societies, children are more likely to be overweight, to be victims of bullying, and to become teenage mothers. Once they become adults in more unequal societies they are more likely to have mental health problems, to have problems with drugs and alcohol, to work longer hours and have more debt pressures on family life. And social mobility is lower in more unequal societies, so it is more difficult for children to escape from intergenerational cycles of poverty and deprivation."

On both accounts, with regard to inequality and child well-being, the US performs extremely dismal compared to other rich countries. (9)
This trend is threatening to become turn into a common pattern in rich(er) and poor(er) countries alike, as being 'born unequal' is clearly related to worrisome disparities in health outcomes.

For example,
> "… disparities in health outcomes do not only exist in poorer countries. In Canada, one of the world's eight richest countries (characterised by deep regional inequalities, with child poverty rates varying from just over 10% to more than twice that), low-income children are 2.5 times more likely to have a problem with vision, hearing, speech or mobility."[v]

29

So while the effects of inequality are there for all to see, pro-market Governments are finding it hard to take off their sunglasses. The platitudes heralded from G8 and G20 summits alike, capture little attention among the working poor and unemployed. First subtle advice to reverse course is now even emerging from within the summiteers' very own policy think tank, namely the OECD.

Perhaps somewhat daringly for a mainstream organization, it has sub-titled a recent publication 'The Role of Empowerment'.

On the cover of the 300-page report, a chain bursts apart, presumably to demonstrate a bold move for "strengthening poor people's organizations, providing them with more control over assets".

The report goes on to observe:
"Globally, extreme and persistent inequalities linked to poverty, gender, ethnicity and language are holding back the development of human capabilities. Policies that successfully counteract such inequalities include improving accessibility and affordability by cutting fees and informal charges; improving quality by providing highly skilled teachers and health workers; expanding entitlements and opportunities by integrating health and education strategies into wider anti-marginalization policies, such as social protection; reinforcing legal entitlements; and supporting a fairer distribution of public spending. "(10)

Word has gotten out earlier still, as few illusions exist among the authors of a 2011 ILO report spell out who question the effectiveness and indeed, the economic relevant of the so-called recovery programs launched so far.

As they point out:

> "The global economic outlook has deteriorated
> significantly since 2010, signaling that the policies
> implemented to date have failed on a number of fronts. ...
> As long-term unemployment rises and workers begin to
> leave the labour market entirely, the window for taking
> decisive action is closing. Urgent action to place
> employment creation at the centre of the recovery plan is
> necessary. "(11)

Such doubts are echoed by UNICEF, which notes that
> "...ironically, while fiscal stimulus packages mainly
> benefited wealthier income groups—not the poor—during
> the first phase of the crisis, budget cuts are
> disproportionately impacting the poor during the second
> phase." (12)

The arguments and statistical evidence demonstrating 'failure by
design' of what is still called the free market, is substantial. Only
protagonists of the status quo, those who either indentify with
the 1% or belong to them (or both), put on a serious face when
defending their 'more of the same' economic medicine, or their
phony potions for economic recovery.

The math is actually quite simple: what the wealthy are given in tax breaks essentially corresponds to wage erosion, limiting of labor benefits and cuts in public services to the unwealthy. In the past year we have all witnessed what has happened in Greece and is now being replicated in Spain, where on top of massive job and income losses, about half of all youth and young workers are now unemployed.

Basically,
" while governments across Europe are making cuts in public expenditure to reduce their deficits, the moral case for proper tax enforcement is particularly strong: every €1,000 of tax that the rich avoid paying, creates the need for another €1,000 of cuts to services to the least well off.

There is an awful inevitability about how the poorest end up paying for the mistakes and dishonesty of the rich whose actions led to the present recession. The scale of tax avoidance among the rich almost begs everyone else to go on a tax strike until the rich are made to pay." (13)

Maintaining profits for the rich remains the unarticulated mantra of the political class as they continue to preach restraint to the masses. The 'we all need to tighten our belts' rhetoric may have subsided under conditions of increasingly blatant inequality as this kind of hollow talk angers more than it consoles. There are more subtle ways, and almost comically creative ones when it comes to squeezing more money out of those who are already living from pay cheque to pay cheque. We probably have all realized that food prices in the supermarket have risen. The ways in which higher prices are passed on are intended to keep consumers in spending mood. New carton designs for your favorite cereal chase the fact that there can be 10 to 15% less cereal inside the box but the price is the same as before.

At the ever-bustling Dollar-stores, what used to be had for a buck now costs $1.25. Basically everywhere else, products displayed as 'On Sale', are nowadays often sold at what used to be the regular price, but are shown as 'normally' having a 20% higher regular price. Many other products now come in smaller packaging while the aisle price is unchanged, creating the illusion of 'stable prices'. Last year a friend of mine bought red bricks for a backyard footpath. When he bought more of them this year to extend the path, he discovered that although the price was unchanged, the bricks were now 2cm shorter.

At school, kids learn nothing of political economy. Instead they are fed half-truths and economic fairytales of how growth produces jobs, told that honest work pays or are led to believe that the 'laws of supply and demand' somehow miraculously determine prices in what is still labeled as a 'free market'.

Our youth are encouraged to accept student loan and credit card debt to drown in: they will be enticed to consume their lives away and buy things that often only meet artificially generated needs and to burden themselves with mortgages until they have retirement in sight. Their kids will hopefully do much of the same it is hoped by the 'business world', in order to keep the lopsided consumer society afloat a little longer.

The notion that everybody pays taxes for public goods and services has turned into little more than a mirage. In fact the richer you are, the less you pay anything that resembles a 'fair share'. Share-issuing companies have adhered to this principle for decades, knowing that if they shift their profits to subsidiaries, frequently based in tax havens, and apply accounting techniques that allow them to demonstrate an annual loss year after year, their tax 'burden' will be zero.

Especially in the US, the 'don't raise taxes' rhetoric is nothing else but the rallying call of the ultra-rich to avoid paying taxes at the rate an average Walmart employee has to pay. Such favourism comes with a hefty price tag for the poor, in terms of declining incomes and reduced or eroding public services:

> "The share of the federal budget funded by corporate income taxes has dropped dramatically since the 1940s, from 28.8 percent of the budget to 10.3 percent.
>
> In 2010, U.S. corporations avoided approximately $60 billion in U.S. corporate income taxes by using a variety of devices and gimmicks to shift profits to foreign subsidiaries, while the Fortune 100 companies received some $89.6 billion in federal contracts. ... major U.S, corporations are avoiding tens of billions of dollars in U.S. corporate income taxes through a variety of devices and gimmicks which allow them to hide profits overseas, often artificially assigning these profits to countries with little or no corporate income tax. (14)

So one can confidently say that the numbers are in, the data is confirmed and the system-discrediting evidence has been produced: inequality is deep and widespread, increasing and worst of all, it is depriving millions of people around the world of decent livelihoods and of hope. Any society that idly stands by or turns a cold shoulder to the politics and economics that create massive inequality is arguably an unethical one. "What to do about it" is a question any decent person will be asking.

 Once this is asked, the central issue of how to change society arises and importantly, the "who" will do something about it needs to be asked. The search for the progressive 'historical subject' is on.

In his well written book, 'The Great Divergence' Tim Noah has addressed many of the inequality concerns also expressed in this article. Disappointingly, the final chapter titled "What We Can Do About It" falls short and does not say who the "we" actually are or to convincingly elaborate on any "how" to overcome today's global inequality. (15)

Ultimately, Noah places hope in benign reforms and technocratic fixes of the system and in those who have historically perpetuated it. He seems at a loss to locate a social counterforce to the ruling economic and political class. Rightfully so, he recognizes the changed frame of mind amongst those who are upset about growing injustices.

Where once anger turned into at times violent political protest and revolt, today, resentment is said to dominate and is often kept inside. I suggest that this might be true for many people; the emergence of the Occupy movement has opened up a multitude of possibilities to oppose, challenge, bypass and undermine the inequality economy. (16)

It is too early to say that the Occupy protests are merely a flare-up of dissent but I would wager that although the movements' intensity and visibility might heavily fluctuate, the desire and preparedness to engage in lasting socioeconomic change is genuine and is bound to have a prolonged, dislodging impact upon the current capitalist political economy.

The people who oppose, object and revolt against the capitalist world of systematic inequality, are of course those posing a serious challenge to capitalism and its' 'business as usual', technocratic and cosmetic approach to dealing not only with economic, but with social and environmental issues as well. It is quite possible that the more radically they (the Occupy movement and its supporters) question and act against the system, the greater their revolutionary impact potentially becomes: within the core capitalist countries and throughout the emerging alternative centers as well as on the economic margins and desolate geographic fringes of what has also been labeled 'armed globalization'.

The ruling classes within free-market preaching states may increasingly fail to compensate for the market failures and environmental and social consequences of unrestrained capitalism. It comes as no surprise that the global governing elites

"..offer only a technical fix to the present (systemic) crisis and have no real…intention of conducting any meaningful radical reform or transformation of the system itself."

But precisely such transformation is needed and is most likely, if indeed at all in the nearer future, to be brought about by
".. all those very people who have been negatively affected by the present system and who, through their lived experiences, realize the need for radical thinking and for radical action" (17)

As 'forces of resistance', these people are likely to continue to form alliances and organize through social networks, and engage in 'conscious collective political action' that challenge the ruling system and unjust distribution of wealth, opportunities and political power. What is fascinating is that with the mobilization of protest and dissent in the Occupy / We are the 99% - movement, indeed such new forms of organizing protest and political action have emerged, facilitated notably through social media (the political outcomes of such mobilization in the wake of the 'Arab Spring', have yet to demonstrate how profoundly they are rooted and based on democratic and socially inclusive aspirations and principles).

In North America and Europe, it has taken many by surprise that a protest movement can in fact be distinctly leaderless: thus representing a stark organizational contrast and alternative to the system-conform efforts of the so-called leaders of our existing, nation states. It is a protest movement, as we have witnessed in Quebec where students have vehemently opposed tuition hikes, which is prepared to ask questions that simply are not asked in the mainstreamed media, such as

"Democracy, as viewed by the other side, is tagged as 'representative' – and we wonder just what it represents." (18)

Spontaneous actions of people who've 'had enough' of being ripped off, of being manipulated by entertainment and consumer industries, or being taken advantage of from the 'cradle to the grave', are finding new ways to express their dissent. As violent conflicts rage outside the borders of our core 'homeland' capitalist countries, living inside the 'free world' has lost much of its meaning for many. The inequalities in the 'land(s) of the free' have definitely become synonymous with 'pursuit of happiness' for those living the good life while floating on their wonderful clouds of luxury, while below, it never stops raining injustices on us common mortals.

© 2013 by Glenn Brigaldino

References

(1) Wikipedia, 2007–2012 global financial crisis,
http://en.wikipedia.org/wiki/Financial_crisis_of_2007%E2%80%932010

(2) Distribution of net worth and financial wealth in the United States,
1983-2007 by G. William Domhoff:
http://www2.ucsc.edu/whorulesamerica/power/wealth.html

(3) THE CRISES OF DEMOCRATIC CAPITALISM, Wolfgang Streeck
in: New Left Review 71 Sept/Oct 2011

(4) Instability Implications of Increasing Inequality - What can be
learned from North America?, Lars Osberg, 2012
**http://www.policyalternatives.ca/publications/reports/instability-
implications-increasing-inequality**

Also see: Of the 1%, by the 1%, for the 1%, Joseph E. Stiglitz, 2011
http://www.vanityfair.com/society/features/2011/05/top-one-percent-
201105#

(5) Sam Pizzigati, Magic Act: Making the Super Rich Disappear, June 2012
'Too Much' commentary of the project of the Program on Inequality and
the Common Good of the D.C.-based Institute for Policy Studies,
http://toomuchonline.org/magic-act-making-the-super-rich-disappear

Also see: The war on salaries - Enough is enough by Sam Pizzigati in
Le Monde diplomatique Feb 2012 "US radicals came up a century ago
with sound proposals for a maximum income, enforced through
progressive taxation, to ensure that the rich couldn't so easily buy
political influence, as well as to adjust inequality ".

(6) Divided We Stand - Why Inequality Keeps Rising, OECD 2011
http://www.oecd.org/document/51/0,3746,en_2649_33933_49147827_1_1
_1_1,00.html
In terms of living standards, it has recently been reported that since
1981, "Canadians experienced a widening of income and wealth
inequalities. There have been poverty reductions, but the reductions
were not nearly as large as the increase in wealth inequality.

See:
Center for the Study of Living Standards, Research Report 2011-17,
Andrew Sharpe and Christopher Ross
http://ideas.repec.org/p/sls/resrep/1117.html

(7) Falling behind: life expectancy in US counties from 2000 to 2007 in
an international context
Sandeep C Kulkarni, Alison Levin-Rector, Majid Ezzati and
Christopher JL Murray Kulkarni et al. Population Health Metrics
2011, 9:16 http://www.pophealthmetrics.com/content/9/1/16

(8) The other crisis: the economics and financing of maternal, newborn
and child health in Asia, Ian Anderson, Henrik Axelson, and B-K Tan,
in: In *Health Policy and Planning, 2010*
http://heapol.oxfordjournals.org/content/26/4/288.long

(9) The Spirit Level: Why Greater Equality Makes Societies Stronger ,
Bill Kerry, Kate E. Pickett and Richard Wilkinson, in:
Child Poverty and Inequality: New Perspectives, Isabel Ortiz, Louise
Moreira Daniels, Sólrún Engilbertsdóttir (Eds), UNICEF, 2012
http://www.unicef.org/socialpolicy/index_62108.html

(10) OECD (2012), Poverty Reduction and Pro-Poor Growth: The Role of
Empowerment;
http://dx.doi.org/10.1787/9789264168350-en
(11) World of work report 2011: Making markets work for jobs /
International Labour Office. 2011

http://www.ilo.org/global/publications/ilo-bookstore/order-
online/books/WCMS_166021/lang--en/index.htm

(12) United Nations Children's Fund (UNICEF), 2012, A Recovery for
All: Rethinking Socio-Economic Policies for Children and Poor
Households, Isabel Ortiz and Matthew Cummins (Editors)

" An analysis of the winners and losers of the crisis must further
consider that, particularly in the economies of the Organisation for
Economic Cooperation and Development (OECD), a large share of
stimulus packages included tax cuts, mainly through reductions in
personal income tax for the wealthy. Thus, ironically, while fiscal
stimulus packages mainly benefited wealthier income groups—not the
poor—during the first phase of the crisis, budget cuts are
disproportionately impacting the poor during the second phase.

The massive bailouts for the financial industry further indicate that the real problem in addressing this global crisis was not the availability of money, but rather the lack of political will. In fact, the amount of money needed annually to achieve the MDGs is a miniscule fraction of the estimated trillions of public money that was mobilized for bank bailouts."
http://www.unicef.org/socialpolicy/index_62107.html

(13) Richard Wilkinson & Kate Pickett in: TAX JUSTICE FOCUS - THE INEQUALITY EDITION THIRD, 2012, issue 2, downloaded from: http://www.newleftproject.org

(14) Corporate America. Untaxed. Tax Avoidance on the Rise. Samuel Kang and Tuan Ngo
http://greenlining.org/resources/pdfs/CorporateAmericaUntaxed.pdf

(15) The Great Divergence: America's Growing Inequality Crisis and What We Can Do about It, Timothy Noah, 2012; Reviewed by Felix Salmon in New York Times:
http://www.mercurynews.com/entertainment/ci_20894263/review-books-from-paul-krugman-and-timothy-noah?source=rss

(16) For an interview Michael Hardt, co-Author of Empire and *Multitude see: Democracy on the Defensive – September/October 2005 issue of Newtopia Magazine, interview conducted by Glenn Brigaldino.*
http://newtopiamagazine.wordpress.com/2012/03/09/archives-democracy-on-the-defensive-interview-with-michael-hardt-co-author-of-empire-and-multitude

(17) Going South: capitalist crisis, systemic crisis, civilisational crisis, Barry Gills in Third World Quarterly: vol. 31, no. 2, pp. 169-184, 2010

This article argues that the current protracted and severe financial and economic crisis is only one aspect of a larger multidimensional set of simultaneous and interacting crises on a global scale. The article constructs an overarching framework of analysis of this unique conjecture of global crises. The three principal crisis aspects are: an economic crisis of (over) accumulation of capital; a world systemic crisis (which includes a global centre-shift in the locus of production, growth and capital accumulation), and a hegemonic transition (which implies long term changes in global governance structures and institutions); and a worldwide civilisational crisis, situated in the socio-historical structure itself, encompassing a comprehensive environmental crisis and the consequences of a lack of correspondence and coherence in the material and ideational structures of world order. In these ways, the global system is now `going south'.

All three main aspects of the global crisis provoke and require commensurate radical social and political responses and self-protective measures, not only to restore systemic stability but to transform the world system.

http://www.tandfonline.com/doi/abs/10.1080/01436591003711926

In **"Days of Destruction, Days of Revolt"** (Knopf, 2012) Chris Hedges and Joe Sacco show in words and drawings what life looks like in places where the marketplace rules without constraints, where human beings and the natural world are used and then discarded to maximize profit. For an upbeat review see Tim Knight at:

http://www.zerohedge.com/contributed/2012-08-05/days-destruction-days-revolt

(18) Share our future – the CLASSE manifesto, reposted by www.OccupyWallSt.org July 14, 2012. The document goes on to note:

This brand of « democracy » comes up for air once every four years, for a game of musical chairs. While elections come and go, decisions remain unchanged, serving the same interests: those of leaders who prefer the murmurs of lobbyists to the clanging of pots and pans.

Each time the people raises its voice in discontent, on comes the answer: emergency laws, with riot sticks, pepper spray, tear gas. When the elite feels threatened, no principle is sacred, not even those principles they preach: for them, democracy works only when we, the people keep our mouths shut.

http://occupywallst.org/article/share-our-future-classe-manifesto

[i] Reuters, September 28, 2012, France Unveils Temporary 75 Percent Super-Rich Tax Rate; in late December 2012, France's constitutional court nixed the new law, as it found technical flaws in it that undermine equal treatment of individuals with households. For example if an individual would make 1.1 million Euros, then he or she would be subject to the 75% rule. However if a household has two or more members each making just shy of 1 million Euros, say 900 thousand, nobody in the household would have to pay the top rate. It is to be expected that the law will be fine-tuned in 2013.

http://www.huffingtonpost.com/2012/09/28/france-tax-rich-rate_n_1922089.html

[ii] BabyCenter®, 2011, How much you'll spend on childcare
http://www.babycenter.com/0_how-much-youll-spend-on-childcare_1199776.bc

[iii] International Labour Organization 2012 Labour in the global South
http://www.ilo.org/global/publications/books/forthcoming-publications/WCMS_187420/lang--en/index.htm

[iv] Official US Poverty Rate Remains High, Middle Class Incomes Decline, September 12, 2012
' Data released by the U.S. Census Bureau today show that, after increasing since 2008, the poverty rate for the U.S. remained stable at 15 percent between 2010 and 2011. Poverty is greatest among children (21.9 percent), compared with seniors (8.7 percent) and working-age adults (13.7 percent).

While poverty remained unchanged, the median annual household income declined for the second year in a row, to $50,054, down 1.5 percent from 2010. '
http://www.sciencenewsline.com/summary/2012091218100024.html

Also see: USA Today, Sept. 14, 2011, Typical U.S. family got poorer during the past 10 years
http://usatoday30.usatoday.com/news/nation/story/2011-09-13/census-household-income/50383882/1

For historical data see: Median Household Income in the United States on Davemanuel.com
http://www.davemanuel.com/median-household-income.php

[v] The Save the Children Fund, 2012, Born Equal - How reducing inequality could give our children a better future
http://www.savethechildren.org.uk/resources/online-library/born-equal

www.ingramcontent.com/pod-product-compliance
Lightning Source LLC
Chambersburg PA
CBHW050844290526

45792CB00002B/520

* 9 7 8 0 9 7 3 3 8 4 7 4 1 *